KIJC

Little Pebble™

Celebrate Winter

All About
Animals
in Winter

by Martha E. H. Rustad

CAPSTONE PRESS
a capstone imprint

Little Pebble is published by Capstone Press,
1710 Roe Crest Drive, North Mankato, Minnesota 56003
www.capstonepub.com

Library of Congress Cataloging-in-Publication Data
Rustad, Martha E. H. (Martha Elizabeth Hillman), 1975– author.
  All about animals in winter / by Martha E. H. Rustad.
     pages cm—(Little pebble. Celebrate winter)
  Summary: "Simple nonfiction text and full-color photographs present animals
in winter"—Provided by the publisher.
  Audience: Ages 5-7
  Audience: K to grade 3
  Includes bibliographical references and index.
  ISBN 978-1-4914-6005-4 (library binding)—ISBN 978-1-4914-6017-7 (pbk.)—
ISBN 978-1-4914-6029-0 (ebook pdf)
  1. Animals—Wintering—Juvenile literature. 2. Animals—Adaptation—
Juvenile literature. 3. Winter—Juvenile literature. I. Title.
  QL753.R87 2016
  591.56—dc23   2015001838

Editorial Credits
Erika L. Shores, editor; Cynthia Della-Rovere, designer;
Tracy Cummins, media researcher; Tori Abraham, production specialist

Photo Credits
FLPA: Robert Canis, 9; Getty Images: John Cancalosi, 19; Shutterstock: ANRi
Photo, 21, Critterbiz, 7, Eric Isselee, 3, Erni, 11, Kellis, 13, Malivan_Iuliia, 5,
nialat, cover, sellingpix, Design Element, stativius, 1, Zolran, 15; SuperStock:
NHPA, 17.

Printed in the United States of America in North Mankato, Minnesota.
032015   008823CGF15

Table of Contents

Finding Food

What do animals do in winter?

Birds visit a feeder.

They eat seeds.

Feathers puff to stay warm.

An owl hunts mice.

It swallows them whole.

A deer scrapes bark.

It eats at dusk and dawn.

A fluffy fox hunts rabbits.

A squirrel stays in its nest.

It eats food it saved.

Winter Rest

Bats sleep in caves.

They rest all winter.

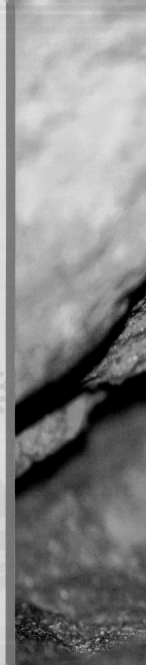

A frog digs under mud.
A frozen frog wakes
in spring.

a wood frog in spring

Bears sleep in dens.

A bear's heart beats slowly.

A bug hides under bark.
It crawls out in spring.

What do you do in winter?

Glossary

bark—the outer layer of a tree trunk

den—an animal home

feeder—a container that holds food for birds; people fill feeders with seeds to feed birds

seed—a tiny plant part from which new plants grow

spring—one of the four seasons of the year; spring is after winter and before summer

winter—one of the four seasons of the year; winter is after fall and before spring

Read More

DeGezelle, Terri. *Exploring Winter*. Exploring the Seasons. North Mankato, Minn.: Capstone Press, 2012.

Gray, Susan H. *Bears Hibernate*. Tell Me Why. Ann Arbor, Mich.: Cherry Lake Publishing, 2015.

Markovics, Joyce. *Wood Frogs*. In Winter, Where Do They Go? New York: Bearport Publishing, 2015.

Internet Sites

FactHound offers a safe, fun way to find Internet sites related to this book. All of the sites on FactHound have been researched by our staff.

Here's all you do:
Visit *www.facthound.com*
Type in this code: 9781491460054

Check out projects, games and lots more at
www.capstonekids.com

Index